UNFORGETTABLE WOMEN OF THE GOSPELS

Unforgettable Women of the Gospels

8 Unnamed Women in Scripture and Their Encounters with Jesus

Melanie Rigney

TWENTY-THIRD PUBLICATIONS
twentythirdpublications.com

THIRD PRINTING 2025

TWENTY-THIRD PUBLICATIONS
977 Hartford Turnpike Unit A
Waterford, CT 06385
(860) 437-3012 or (800) 321-0411
www.twentythirdpublications.com

ISBN: 978-1-62785-790-1
Printed in the U.S.A.

bayard A division of Bayard, Inc.

DEDICATION

To Sara Sullivan and Kathleen Kelley Hofer

The world may not know

your names, but He does—

and I am blessed that I do.

CONTENTS

INTRODUCTION

We don't know their names—but Jesus did. He knew all about them. They didn't have to tell him what had happened to them in the past; his focus was on where they were when their paths crossed and on sharing love, mercy, and the hope of salvation.

Some of these encounters—such as his observation of the widow's offering at the temple—are brief. Others—such as the woman at the well and the woman with the alabaster jar—are quite lengthy.

Each encounter is profound in its own way, with its own lesson for Jesus' followers then and today. One, the woman whose daughter had an unclean spirit, may have even had a lesson for Jesus himself.

Each chapter begins with the relevant Scripture and some cross-references you may find useful. Next, we will look at each woman's story and how she might have felt at the time of the encounter. These emotions might include hope, fear, faith, and desperation. Many had tried everything else before approaching

Jesus. Maybe you find yourself in a similar crisis, going to Jesus as your last rather than first resort. I understand; I've been there.

I've provided a few thoughts on what could have happened to the woman after the encounter. I'd love to think they all became great evangelists within their families and communities and never tired of testifying about their experiences and Jesus' greatness, wouldn't you? But we don't really know. Time passes, and memories and emotions fade. That happens to us today. God's grace is given freely, but unless we chronicle them in some way—an ongoing prayer of gratitude, perhaps, or something tangible like a journal entry, a photo, a scrapbook page—the power of even our most profound Jesus moments can dwindle.

You will also find a section about what Jesus may want us to take away from this encounter for our own lives. We may not have to tote water from a well, or be involved in an adulterous relationship, but these women's situations writ large are eternal: Rejection by society. Chronic illness. Loss. Poverty.

I've also included a story from my life when I received or observed grace occurring in a similar way. A good friend of mine's writing mantra is "Unzip your soul and expose your foibles." And sisters, I have foibles aplenty.

In researching this book, I came across some profound insights into each woman's story: from a pope, priest, or minister. One "Deeper Dive" appears with each chapter, along with the writer's name and where you can view the full homily or sermon.

The story of a "forgotten" woman saint whose life echoes the unnamed woman's journey is also shared.

Each chapter closes with three discussion questions appropriate for individual or group study, an action item (such as a journaling or scrapbooking prompt), and a prayer.

The unnamed women who encountered Jesus two thousand years ago didn't live in a world of viral videos and social media shaming, but make no mistake—like us, they knew about judgment and ostracization and the price that accepting grace and changing carries. Regardless of what they did after the encounter, their stories have inspired people for generations. These women are unforgettable.

Similarly, our names may not be known to the world, but sharing our encounters with the Lord can change hearts and souls. Let's get started.

1

The Widow's Offering

GIVING ALL WE HAVE

He sat down opposite the treasury and watched the crowd putting money into the treasury. Many rich people put in large sums. A poor widow came and put in two small copper coins, which are worth a penny. Then he called his disciples and said to them, "Truly I tell you, this poor widow has put in more than all those who are contributing to the treasury. For all of them have contributed out of their abundance, but she out of her poverty has put in everything she had, all she had to live on." ◆ **MARK 12:41–44**

Her Story

It is the day she comes to tithe. She doesn't have much; she never does. How she would get by without those precious coins, she isn't sure. But she brings them anyway. She is so focused on her concerns that she pays little attention to the teacher or the large crowd.

Jesus has just finished denouncing the scribes, indicting them because they are more interested in their own prominence in society than in anyone or anything elsewhere. Oh, they pray—at length—but they "devour widows' houses." Jesus then sits opposite the treasury and observes those who are making donations.

> **Cross-References**
>
> **MARK 12:38–40**
> *Jesus denounces those who give for the sake of appearances*
>
> **2 CORINTHIANS 9:6–7**
> *Give generously and cheerfully*
>
> **MATTHEW 19:27**
> *Peter says the disciples have given everything and asks what they will have*

Today, we make our donations to the parish electronically or when the basket comes around during Mass. Temple donations in Jerusalem were made in a more elaborate, public form. The treasury consisted of thirteen chests. Two were for the annual tax that every Jewish man over the age of twenty paid to help with the temple upkeep. The tax was said to have amounted to a couple of days' wages. The other eleven chests were for other offerings, each for a specific purpose—purification, for example, or a burnt or sin offering. The chests were shaped like shofars, or trumpets, wide at the bottom and narrowing toward the top. All the chests were located in the Court of the Women; all purified Jews, men and women, could enter that court.

This is where Jesus sits after his criticism of the scribes. It's a busy day; a crowd of people are coming and going, and "many rich people put in large sums" (Mark 12:41). But Jesus watches one woman in particular. Likely, he knows she is a widow by her clothing; the quality of the fabric indicates that she is not wealthy. Perhaps the scribes had "devoured" her house. Perhaps the couple's savings had been eaten up by charlatans who promised to cure her husband and could not. It would seem there were no adult children to help her. A late-nineteenth-century painting by the French artist James Tissot shows the woman walking away, carrying a young child in her arms, with Jesus and the others watching her. A well-dressed man is making an offering in the background, and similarly dressed men wait behind him to do the same. A modern-day depiction by Darren Gygi shows the woman about to drop her coins into the treasury as a dirty-faced girl holds onto her mother's skirt.

Regardless of how the widow came to her current state in life, when she reaches the treasury, she puts in two pennies. That's what this woman had to give. A couple of pennies, the least valuable Roman coin. Many of us don't even stop to pick up a penny on the sidewalk these days; it's just not worth our while.

Jesus doesn't stop her, doesn't offer a "well done, good and faithful servant." She may not even have heard his words as she walked away.

It is the last time we see Jesus in the temple before he gives his all for us.

WHAT HAPPENED TO THE WOMAN?

Unlike many of the women in this Bible study, the widow wasn't healed by Jesus and didn't see someone who was. She doesn't even have a conversation with him and may or may not have heard his words extolling her as an example.

I like to think she *did* hear his words about her. And while she didn't turn around and thank him or ask for help, perhaps hearing his words brought her some solace—and she kept on offering all she had, financially, physically, and spiritually.

WHAT WE CAN LEARN FROM THE WOMAN

Not long before Jesus and his followers leave for the Passover in Jerusalem, a young man asks Jesus what he must do to have eternal life beyond keeping the commandments. Jesus' answer is not an easy one: "go, sell your possessions, and give the money to the poor, and you will have treasure in heaven; then come, follow me" (Matthew 19:21). After the young man goes away, having chosen his possessions over eternal life, Jesus remarks that it will be hard for those with wealth to enter the kingdom. Peter is flummoxed, saying, "Look, we have left everything and followed you. What then will we have?" (Matthew 19:27).

Does Jesus really want us to give away everything—all our time, talent, and treasure? Can we truly be assured of a place in heaven if we do that? What's the bare minimum: tithing two percent, an hour a month of good works, and fifteen minutes a day in prayer? And what will we have if we do, other than less money in the bank, less time with TikTok and Candy Crush, and fewer public accolades? What then will we have?

We may laugh a little and shake our heads at the brazenness of Peter's question, in essence making faith transactional, a quid pro quo. But in our souls, we know we ask the same question and offer bargains that are even more impudent: Cure my mother's cancer, and I'll go to Mass more regularly. Give me that new job, and I'll give my parish more money. Send someone who will pay what I want for my latest sculpture, and I'll give free lessons at the community center. If our offer isn't accepted, we think God is unfair and turn away. If the cancer is cured, the new job is offered, someone buys the sculpture, we forget about what we promised to do in exchange. Rinse, spit, repeat.

It's the story of the human condition: we don't expect something for nothing. We just want that "something" to be on our own terms. And in that, we can learn much from the widow. She may have wailed to God in her darkest moments about why her husband was taken away and why she had nothing but those two coins. But her faith carried her past the wailing. She gave all she had and left without calling attention to herself. She was obedient. That is all God desires of us. It requires us to swallow our own wants and needs and will in favor of the Almighty's. It is everything.

A Story
Learning to Give

I'm a cradle Catholic who left any kind of faith shortly before my sixteenth birthday and returned to full communion in the Church when I was forty-nine. My return coincided, perhaps not surprisingly, with hitting rock bottom. I had been fired in a management change from a job I loved and had taken a position in the federal government in a city five hundred miles away where I knew a total of two people. I left behind an estranged husband who had amassed a quarter of a million dollars in credit card debt.

As I was returning to faith, I filed for bankruptcy, which meant I repaid more than $100,000 of that debt in three years. At the beginning of that time, my take-home pay was less than a thousand dollars a month, and that didn't go very far in 2005 in the Washington, DC, area. I did a lot of freelance editing at nights and on weekends, but I likely wouldn't have made it if one of my sisters hadn't moved to the area and become my roommate.

I was very grateful to God for showing me love and mercy, and a good share of what was left after the rent and utilities went to my parish. It wasn't much, maybe fifty dollars some months. But it truly was all I had. And God took care of me.

As my take-home pay grew, so did my financial generosity. That was easy. I've lived on almost nothing, after all. But I am not so generous with giving God my time.

In March 2020, I had been praying the Divine Office most days for two months. I was co-facilitating a weekly women's Bible study group. I was praying the Rosary most evenings before I went to bed.

But then COVID came. And while you would have thought that having all that time when things were shut down would have greatly enhanced my prayer practice and time with God, the opposite became true. We had to end the Bible study and, at that point, electronic options weren't as available as they are now. My day job routine changed so that finding those ten or twenty minutes in the morning and throughout the day became "impossible." At least, that's what I told myself. I still prayed the Rosary each night, but mostly, as a priest once put it to me, "the angels finished it."

A nearby parish brought back an early Sunday morning Mass with distancing and masking the following January, and I was slammed in the face with the reason I had returned to faith: to be fed by the Eucharist. While it had been fun to attend virtual Masses in France, Ireland, Canada, England, Scotland, and Malaysia, for me it wasn't really Mass without the Eucharist. Jesus was giving me his all, but I still was squeezing him in on my terms.

In the spring of 2023, I attended a three-day retreat on authenticity. I planned to spend most of it writing this book. But the first evening, the speaker talked about trust: "Whom can we trust to tell us who we really are? Can we trust ourselves? Our friends? Our enemies? TV commercials? Let's listen to the one who knows best—the one who made us." Then she gave us some lovely Scripture verses about God's love for us. After the reflection, I spent many hours thinking about trusting God. Love God? Of course. Attempt to be obedient? Of course. Trust God? Hmmm.

I realized that I had lost that woman who gave what she had—almost nothing—when she took her first halting steps back to Mass in the late summer of 2005. I trusted God then because I had nowhere else to turn. And the Almighty graciously accepted the mess that I was and welcomed me with open arms. I had been deluding myself that if I was a generous giver monetarily, it didn't matter whether I was still giving my all in faith.

I am now working my way back to trust. I have some sympathy for the scribes Jesus calls out in Mark 12. Maybe I wasn't bragging about what I give financially, as they were, but I was holding back in another important way—time. Strange as it seems to me, I'm relearning that the Lord actually desires to spend time with me. He wants more than my money, more than volunteering. He. Wants. Time. With Me. Imperfect, messy me.

I recently ran across this quote from Thomas Merton: "In order to become myself I must cease to be what I always wanted to be." I'd take that a step further: In order to become myself, I must cease to be what *I* think God wants and trust that the Lord will illumine who I am to become. That can be the most difficult gift of all for us to give the Lord—our trust.

A Deeper Dive

"He sees even this poor widow, whom others brush past with haste or contempt. He knows her struggle and sacrifice and single-heartedness, as she brings that tiny offering, with a blush of shame that it is so little, and secretly lets it fall into the treasury of her God. His condescension is still displayed to the meanest and the humblest worshipers, and broken words, paltry gifts, and feeble efforts will not be without his notice and recompense."
A. ROWLAND[4]

Putting in Everything She Had
Saint Lucy Pak Hiu-sun (1801–1839)

In 1984, Pope John Paul II traveled to Seoul to canonize ninety-three Koreans and ten French missionaries who died for their faith between 1839 and 1867. Among the best known was Andrew Kim Taegon, the first Korean-born Catholic priest, who was just twenty-five years old when he was tortured and beheaded in 1846.

Lucy Pak Hiu-sun's name is seldom invoked when we talk about our glorious martyrs, and that's a shame. For just as the widow Jesus lauded offered everything she had, so did Lucy.

Lucy was born into Korean nobility. She was known not only for her beauty, but also for her well-formed mind. She studied in both Korean and Chinese. That combination led to fifteen years of service at the royal palace, including time as a lady-in-waiting to Queen Sunwon, who was just a year younger than Lucy. Lucy was also politically adept; she managed to fend off the king's advances and remain in the queen's good graces.

She was about thirty when she heard the gospel proclaimed for the first time. This Jesus and his teachings were a revelation to Lucy and came at a moment when she had begun to question the excesses of palace life. A role at the palace was both highly valued and difficult to leave alive, but Lucy convinced people that she was ill and so was allowed to go.

But to where? Her father would not accept her, given her budding dangerous views. She eventually moved in with a nephew, renouncing her fine clothing and other trappings. Her example was so moving that her nephew and his family converted to Catholicism, as did her older sister when she joined the household.

The year 1839 brought an edict severely limiting the practice of Catholicism; later in the year, it was outlawed entirely in Korea. It was in this climate that Lucy went out to greet the authorities, offering them food and wine, when they arrived at the house on April 1. She said it was God's will they had arrived, so they should be welcomed.

Lucy had given much for Jesus before her martyrdom—her social standing, her beautiful clothes, many of her family relationships. It is said that Lucy's torture was worse than the women with whom she was imprisoned, the authorities' logic being that she had betrayed the law and the court in converting. Along with eight others, she gave her all and was beheaded on May 24, 1839.

Unforgettable You

CONTEMPLATION

Think about or discuss:

- What do you think happened to the widow who gave all she had? What might her life have been like five or ten years after this day?
- Why didn't Jesus ask the woman to stop and talk with him? How might her life had been affected if he had?
- What have you given up for Jesus, tangibly or intangibly? What is he asking you to give him that you'd rather keep—and why do you want to keep it? This may not be money, but perhaps time or forgiveness or grace to someone you find difficult to be around, much less love.

ACTION

Look at the James Tissot or Darren Gygi paintings of the widow, or find another depiction. Journal about your thoughts about the widow or others who are shown. Or gather images of what giving your all for Christ means to you.

PRAYER

Jesus, I am not good at giving my all
for you; there are possessions I would
rather keep, even though I know they
get in the way of my loving you.
There are wounds I would rather
let fester than bring them to you
for healing. Please help me to unclutch
my hands from these things
and offer myself completely to you.
Amen.

2

The Widow at Nain

FINDING LIFE IN DEATH

Soon afterward he went to a town called Nain, and his disciples and a large crowd went with him. As he approached the gate of the town, a man who had died was being carried out. He was his mother's only son, and she was a widow, and with her was a large crowd from the town. When the Lord saw her, he was moved with compassion for her and said to her, "Do not cry." Then he came forward and touched the bier, and the bearers stopped. And he said, "Young man, I say to you, rise!" The dead man sat up and began to speak, and Jesus gave him to his mother. ◆ **LUKE 7:11–15**

Her Story

The widow has contemplated her future, and it is bleak.

Her husband is dead, and now so is her only son. That leaves her, in essence, alone. The townspeople care enough about her that they join the funeral procession—she certainly couldn't afford to hire mourners and musicians the way wealthy people did. That show of support had to have brought the widow some comfort. But it was unlikely that any of them would take her into their homes. By tradition, she would become the responsibility of a distant relative—if she had one.

Cross-References

1 KINGS 17
Elijah revives the widow's son

2 KINGS 4:8–37
Elisha raises the Shunammite woman's son from the dead

EPHESIANS 2:1–8
Those in the world are dead due to sins; Christ died to bring us back to life

Where will she go? Who will she rely on? Thoughts and fears of what was to come likely intermingled with her deep grief and sorrow. Her son, the light of her life, could have died from an unnamed cause the very same day. She may have already ripped her garments on the right side of her chest to show the depth of her devastation.

By tradition, the widow was at the head of the funeral procession. Perhaps that is a good thing, for it meant that her son's bier—the simple open pallet on which the body is being carried—is behind her. She won't have to gaze on his shroud-wrapped body or see it jostled about as the men carry it. This is another sign of the widow's poverty: that a more elaborate conveyance is not being used to take the son to the burial site. It will be a sad, painful walk of about ten miles. (Archaeologists have found a site east of the town from that era.)

She and the other mourners are near the edge of town when they encounter a crowd of people coming in. The contrast in emotion is great; this group is ebullient because the day before, they were in Capernaum with Jesus when he healed the centurion's gravely ill servant without even seeing the man. They also likely are tired—it's a thirty-mile uphill journey from Capernaum to Nain. But tradition holds that they will join the funeral procession, even if they didn't know the young man.

The paths of Jesus and the widow have not crossed before. This is his first trip to Nain during his public ministry, and only Luke describes it. But the wretchedness of the woman's situation and her sobs move Jesus.

"Do not cry," he tells her.

Do not cry?

She has lost her beloved only son and the only means of support left to her. She is devastated. How could she stop the tears? *Why* would she stop the tears?

Jesus touches the bier, and the crowd goes silent. This is not done. In their eyes, this act has made him unclean. Whether they are his followers or part of the original funeral procession, this is odd—for some, even shocking.

What happens next is even more extraordinary. Jesus tells the son to rise.

And the son sits up and begins to talk. Jesus gives him to his mother.

We are told that those in the crowd are in awe and glorify God, calling Jesus a great prophet. The mother? Imagine the shock and joy coursing through her. A day earlier, her son was alive. Then he was dead. Now, he has been returned to her in a way that is beyond her comprehension. But she knows he is alive again: he is talking with her, and his flesh is warm when she touches him. How did all this happen?

WHAT HAPPENED TO THE WOMAN?

One would like to think that at some point in each remaining day of her life and, certainly, anytime she looked at her son, she remembered this miraculous day.

Perhaps the event sparked formation of a community of believers, and perhaps she became a matriarch for the group, encouraging them and reminding them of what they had seen. Or perhaps she went home, grateful but unchanged, and cared for her son and, later, his wife and children.

WHAT WE CAN LEARN FROM THE WOMAN

Jesus does a great deal of healing in the gospels, but only on three occasions does he bring back people from physical death: the widow's son; Jairus' daughter; and Lazarus. The raising of the widow's son in particular hearkens back to two Old Testament passages: Elijah's revival of the widow of Zarephath's son in 1 Kings 17, and Elisha's raising of the Shunammite woman's son in 2 Kings 4:8–37.

In the case of Elijah, a drought has descended upon the land because God is displeased with the people. Elijah has been told to leave Israel and its toxic rulers and is sent to Zarephath (now the Lebanese town of Sarafand), where God tells him a widow will feed him. He finds the woman preparing a final meal for herself and her son before they die of starvation. She makes him a cake, as Elijah asks, and the household survives for many days. Then the son becomes deathly ill. Elijah stretches himself over the son three times and prays, and the child is revived.

Elisha, Elijah's successor, has a meal with a family in Shunem and foretells that they will be blessed with a son. Some years later, the son dies in his mother's lap. She lays him on the bed Elisha uses when he visits and goes in search of Elisha. The two of them return to the Shunammite woman's home, and Elisha prays, bends over the son and in essence performs mouth-to-mouth resuscitation, and the child returns to life.

We find great similarities among the three stories, but also great differences. In the case of the widow of Nain's son, Jesus does not pause to pray to the Almighty; we see him capable of bringing people back to life on his own, signaling his divinity. Heroic physical efforts on Jesus' part are not necessary; he simply touches the bier.

Shunem is less than ten miles from today's Nain. Sarafand is a couple of hundred miles further north, but none of the three is memorable to the world for much beyond these biblical miracles. Nain, now known as Nein or Nin, is a town of about two thousand people about four miles from Mount Tabor and eight miles southeast of Nazareth.

Even for pilgrims, Nain, which means "green pastures" or "gracefulness," is as off the beaten path today as it was two thousand years ago. There's a highway exit sign with "Widow's Son" in three languages; the exit also has a gas station and fast-food restaurant. A small church originally built during the Crusades and rebuilt by the Franciscans in 1880 is still open by appointment.

But all three sons in 1 Kings, 2 Kings, and Luke had one thing in common, as did Jairus' daughter and Lazarus: while they were all given additional time on earth, they would all die one day. And mothers and fathers, spouses, children, and other loved ones would mourn and cry.

"Do not cry," Jesus told the widow at Nain. He was not telling her to pick up her cross and follow daily. He was not telling her about the possibility of eternal life for his followers. The latter would become clear soon enough, when Jesus, another widow's son, would himself die to redeem us all. In the moment, Jesus is promising the woman comfort. And he delivered, far beyond anything she could have prayed for. He raised her son from the dead; he raised her heart and soul from despair. Which was the greater gift that day?

The people of Nain were wrong about one thing. Jesus was not just a great prophet in the manner of Elijah and Elisha. They were seeing God the Son himself that day. And with Jesus, we know where we're going, who cares for us, who will dry our tears, and who desires to have us with him for eternity. Without him, we are as destitute and desperate as the widow of Nain was when the funeral procession began. Death will not be the victor unless we believe it can be.

A Story
Finding Life in Death

I got a call on the evening of October 8, 1988. The daughter of a former boss and four other seventh-grade girls had died in a peaceful Wisconsin village after being hit by a car. They were walking to a birthday party. Later, we would all learn that the seventeen-year-old boy who was driving the car had had an epileptic seizure, even though he faithfully took his medication; no charges were ever filed.

It couldn't be! The last time I had seen Nicole, she was a tow-headed six-year-old who loved to laugh and play dress-up.

Four days later, my husband and I and a former colleague drove the two hundred miles from Chicago to attend the funeral of Nicole and two of the other girls. The three little white coffins were almost too much to bear. So was the world's interest in the tragedy, even for news veterans; national reporters were everywhere, and President Reagan sent a note of personal condolences.

Dozens of us went to the family home after the funeral. My former boss was bleary-eyed and rambling, crying at some points. His wife said little; she just sat, looking shell-shocked. It was hard for most of us to find words or do anything other than hug them both and each other.

It was their other daughter, Kendra, still in her teens, who held us all together. She was the gracious hostess, asking people's names and making sure everyone had drinks and food.

Someone asked Kendra how she could do all this; the two sisters had always been close. "Yes, it's awful," Kendra responded, "but I have faith she's happy and with Jesus now."

It didn't make sense then that a teenager was confident enough of the hope of eternal life to both mourn and celebrate her little sister. Thirty-five years on, it still doesn't make total sense to me. But sometimes, I think of Kendra when I read stories about saints who were unafraid of death while their bodies or hearts were being broken. Like them, Kendra would not let tragedy take her eyes off the Lord.

A Deeper Dive

"Receiving him from Jesus' hands she becomes a mother for the second time, but the son who is now restored to her is not the one who received life from her. Mother and son thus receive their respective identities thanks to the powerful word of Jesus and to his loving gesture."

POPE FRANCIS, AUGUST 10, 2016[5]

Finding Life in Death:
Saint Angela of Foligno (1248–1309)

Francis of Assisi. Clare of Assisi. Benedict of Nursia. Rita of Cascia. Chances are, if you look at a map of Italy's Umbria region, those are the first four saints who come to mind. Great saints and inspirations all, of course, but we can also learn much from another saint of the area, the mystic Angela of Foligno, who was canonized by Pope Francis in 2013.

Little was remarkable about Angela's early life. Like other wealthy young women of her time in her central Italian community, she had a modicum of education, married, enjoyed fine clothing and food, and loved to gossip. Her widowed mother encouraged her focus on worldliness, which does not appear to have been slowed down by the arrival of several sons. Angela's behavior wasn't particularly scandalous. But it also didn't allow much room for God other than Mass attendance.

In her thirties, Angela slowly became more introspective. Some of this self-examination may have begun because of outside events: a major earthquake hit her hometown on April 30, 1279. Foligno was frequently at war with neighboring cities. It was against this backdrop in 1285 that Angela prayed fervently for the gift of a suitable confessor to help with her budding spirituality and was visited by Saint Francis of Assisi. (Francis had died about ten miles from Foligno in 1226 and, in one of the fastest canonizations ever, had been declared a saint less than two years later.) The next day, Angela found her confessor.

Not long after, the Holy Spirit spoke to Angela about God's love as she was en route to Saint Francis Basilica in Assisi. Other mystical experiences involved Jesus and the Blessed Virgin.

Angela began ridding herself of her most beautiful possessions as a result of these visions. She lost even more in 1288: everyone in her immediate family died—her husband, all their sons, and her mother (whom she referred to in her *Book of Visions and Instructions* as "a great obstacle to me in the way of God"). There would be no miraculous raising from the dead of these relatives. Angela acknowledged that while she grieved these losses, she took consolation in her faith.

In 1291, Angela became a Franciscan tertiary and later founded a community of sisters. While they took religious vows, they were novel for the time in that they were not enclosed in a convent but were active in ministry. She called her followers "her children," and they called her "Mother."

Unforgettable You

CONTEMPLATION

Think about or discuss:

- What do you think happened to the widow of Nain? What might her life have been like five or ten years after this day?
- Identify a time when you felt very close to Jesus due to a grace granted. Has that experience changed the way you interact with people today—or not? Has time caused this connection to fade? If so, what could you do to rekindle it?
- Angela of Foligno's conversion may have been sparked in part by a war and an earthquake. How has the COVID-19 pandemic or gun violence or a natural disaster such as wildfires, flooding, or a hurricane tested or enhanced your faith in the past five years?

ACTION

Find a favorite picture of yourself with one of your parents, perhaps on a sacramental occasion. A photo with a spiritual parent is fine too! Consider writing a prayer or note of thanks or assemble a collage of these times.

PRAYER

Jesus, you healed the heart
of the widow at Nain when you raised
up her son and restored her hope.
Please open my heart to your
healing balm. Amen.

3

The Woman Healed on the Sabbath

SETTING US FREE FROM OUR AILMENTS

Now he was teaching in one of the synagogues on the Sabbath. And just then there appeared a woman with a spirit that had crippled her for eighteen years. She was bent over and was quite unable to stand up straight. When Jesus saw her, he called her over and said, "Woman, you are set free from your ailment." When he laid his hands on her, immediately she stood up straight and began praising God. But the leader of the synagogue, indignant because Jesus had cured on the Sabbath, kept saying to the crowd, "There are six days on which work ought to be done; come on those days and be cured and not on the Sabbath day." But the Lord answered him and said, "You hypocrites! Does not each of you on the Sabbath untie his ox or his donkey from the manger and lead it to water? And ought not this woman, a daughter of Abraham whom Satan bound for eighteen long years, be set free from this bondage on the Sabbath day?" When he said this, all his opponents were put to shame, and the entire crowd was rejoicing at all the wonderful things being done by him. ◆ **LUKE 13:10–17**

Cross-References

GENESIS 17:7
God's covenant with Abraham

JOB 1:20–22
After the loss of his sons and daughter, Job still praises the Lord

2 CORINTHIANS 1:3–6
God consoles us in our afflictions

Her Story

It took her a long time to get to the temple's Court of the Women, even though she didn't live far away.

Walking was a challenge, had been for eighteen years, though it seemed the pain was at its worst when she was still. It was impossible to stand erect. She had to peer ahead to see if other people were coming by looking for their feet or hearing their voices or the rustling of their clothing. She sometimes thought of her childhood and how she took for granted looking at the sky and seeing people's smiles.

Long ago, she had become used to the whispers: "What's wrong with that woman? Why is she like that?" It seems likely her condition stemmed from a disease; if an accident had caused her to be unable to stand, the townspeople would have known that. Similarly, the religious authorities could not have believed her condition resulted from demonic possession; after all, she was allowed in the synagogue to worship. The people in the town may have known her name, but one wonders how often she heard it in public. Still, she was a woman of faith, a daughter of Abraham, and the whispers would not keep her from worship.

This time, she was going to hear a teacher. Maybe she'd heard him before out on the streets, or maybe she had overheard others talking about his words of divine love and the coming of the kingdom.

The woman probably didn't expect anything other than some wisdom to chew over in her head. In the early days, she had spent a lot of time, money, and hope on people who said they could cure her. None of them did, though they were all happy to keep her money.

She cautiously entered the temple's Court of the Women and waited in her usual spot, perhaps in a corner where others wouldn't stare at her. She wouldn't be able to see this Jesus, but that was fine. She just wanted to hear the lesson.

Then he noticed her.

She couldn't see his face or his eyes, but she could feel his warm gaze. He asked her to come forward. It was clear he could be talking about no one else.

The woman shuffled past other feet to the sound of his voice. She cocked her head as best she could; she wanted to see this man. He was different; his beautiful eyes met her. They were eyes of compassion, not pity.

"Woman, you are set free from your ailment," he said calmly. Then he touched her, and suddenly she could stand! There was no pain! She could see other people's eyes; some, especially the synagogue leader's, looked frightened.

But she could stand! There was no pain! Praise poured out of her.

The woman had a dim sense of the leader questioning why her healing had come on the Sabbath, and the teacher, to the delight of others in the temple, arguing that she was as worthy of relief on the Sabbath as the leader's livestock. But it was only a dim sense. Her focus was on gratitude for the healing.

WHAT HAPPENED TO THE WOMAN?

Biblical scholars believe the woman likely suffered from ankylosing spondylitis, a chronic inflammatory rheumatic disease that usually starts with low back pain and stiffness. Then and today, there is no cure; medication typically is used for pain management and to slow the disease's progression.

Such a recovery of full body motion would be miraculous even today. Once healed, the woman likely was able to resume or perform for the first time in years the activities of any other first-century woman her age.

It's safe to say that at least in the short term, she remembered Jesus and his healing every time she got up in the morning, took a step, had a face-to-face conversation, went about her daily tasks, ate meals, and went to bed at night.

WHAT WE CAN LEARN FROM THE WOMAN

Most of the homilies and the writings on this healing focus on Jesus' exchange with the synagogue leader, and rightly so. The leader tells the crowd that Jesus could have cured the woman on any other day of the week: the Sabbath is a day of rest. Jesus says that even livestock are relieved of their bondage on the Sabbath, so why should not the woman be set free from her bondage on that day?

Jesus does thirty-seven miracles before his crucifixion, and only a handful come on the Sabbath. The point, as Jesus says in Mark 2:27–28, is that "The Sabbath was made for humankind and not humankind for the Sabbath, so the Son of Man is lord even of the Sabbath." Jesus is not a great prophet; he is the Divine. And as difficult as the religious leadership seems to find it, their carefully studied rules did not apply to him. This woman's healing was a sanctification, not a magic show, and was most worthy of the Sabbath.

But when we look only at the Sabbath debate, we miss out on a beautiful bit of Jesus' compassion—and the woman's faith.

She didn't waylay Jesus as he entered, begging for relief from her state. There's no indication she went to the temple that day in search of a miracle. Maybe she hadn't heard the stories; maybe she was resigned to her situation and believed it would never change. And perhaps that is part of the reason Jesus noticed her.

Take note of the language Jesus uses. While he addresses her as "Woman," a term of respect we see him use with his own mother, when he speaks to the synagogue leader, he calls her a "daughter of Abraham." Not "the woman who can't stand up straight," or something worse. A valued daughter of the man with whom God made the covenant.

Even the language about her condition is different than in Mark 1:23–26, when Jesus, at the Capernaum synagogue, calls out the "unclean spirit" from the man. This is an adult woman who is not bedridden or completely incapacitated. This is no exorcism; a demon hasn't taken up residence in her. Jesus speaks to her directly of healing; he does not command a demon to leave. Jesus talks of her being bound by Satan, not possessed, and that's a big difference. The devil attempts to bind us all in all sorts of ways here on earth, but that binding cannot be permanent if we trust not in his evil but in God's mercy and love.

Instead, the words are similar to those Jesus uses in the healing of the man born blind in John 9:3, whom Jesus says was born thus "so that God's works might be revealed in him."

There are many beautiful lessons in this miracle. For ourselves, we can take comfort and courage in the fact that the woman was cured even though she didn't ask for healing. And after eighteen years, she was cured immediately, not in stages, much as we are when we make a full and truthful confession and receive the sacrament of penance and reconciliation.

The greater challenge for us, perhaps, is Jesus' directness. He sees a need and stops in the middle of his teaching to address it. Not after he finishes, not by asking her to meet him the following day (wouldn't that have made the synagogue leader happy!). In the same way, when we are presented with an opportunity to heal in his name, be it twenty minutes with a grieving friend, contributing to a fund for victims of a natural disaster, or giving our skills to a parish project that will be in peril without our assistance, consider a yes rather than an "after I check my calendar" or "I'll have to see; I'm so busy." We may never understand their afflictions, or our own, for that matter. But by helping people when we see the need, we please the Lord and help him help us.

Due to her disease, the woman could only look down—at the ground, at the things of earth. Her presence at the temple, however, could indicate she also knew how to look up with what Paul called the eyes of the heart. Sometimes we need help to open those eyes.

A Story
Setting Free

I grew up in a time when figures of authority were, well, figures of authority. So, when my mother asked my third-grade teacher if she thought there was something wrong with my eyes—both she and Dad wore glasses—Mrs. Ellwein told her I'd tested fine, but I had this nervous habit of getting up to throw away paper tissues in the garbage can near the blackboard every hour or so.

Silly me! I thought that was how everyone read what was on the blackboard: by getting up close to it.

That summer, my parents took me to the optometrist. It turned out I was legally blind. Fortunately, my vision was correctable. Once I had glasses, I was never without them; I even wore them to bed sometimes in the early days. I never really thought of my acute myopia as a burden or a punishment; I just chalked it up to genetics and was grateful for glasses.

But my soul also can be myopic, as I learned in 2009. It was the year after I'd experienced a detached retina while traveling in Turkey. I talked with my ophthalmologist about seeing flashing lights before I left. He did a cursory check and said I had nothing to worry about. He was almost as cavalier the day I came home from Turkey and made a beeline for his office a few hours later; he hadn't bothered to read my chart to see which eye was having problems.

Fortunately, he sent me to an excellent retinal practice, and fifteen years later, I'm still a happy patient there. The reattachment went better than even the retina specialist thought was possible, and my vision remains perfect in that eye.

A few days after the surgery, the ophthalmologist called me. I hung up on him rather than start yelling. He contacted the retina specialist to accuse him of poisoning the relationship. I wrote the ophthalmologist a letter detailing the ways he had failed me, and I sent a copy to the retina specialist.

The following spring, I had a routine follow up with the retina specialist. I went on and on about who would have thought it: my detachment turned out to be a good thing. He agreed—and then said since I felt that way and it was Lent, maybe it was time for me to write another letter.

Call it a blind spot. It had never occurred to me that the ophthalmologist might have felt awful about everything that had happened and that even if he didn't, I needed to extend him mercy. So, I wrote that second letter, telling him how well everything had gone and saying that I forgave him.

I never heard back from the ophthalmologist. But I felt healed, nonetheless. Thanks, Jesus.

Being Set Free from Ailments:
Saint Margaret of Castello (1287–1320)

More than four hundred years passed between Margaret's beatification and her canonization in April 2021. It's easy to see why her story might be forgotten, but it's also easy to see why it's important to remember her.

Margaret was blind from birth. She grew to be only four feet tall, with one leg an inch and a half shorter than the other. A curvature of the spine meant she would never walk normally. Charitably, Margaret's noble Italian family might have worried that the devil had marked her at birth. Less charitably, her mother and father may have been embarrassed by her disabilities.

The parents kept Margaret from almost everyone. When she was six, her existence was almost discovered. In response, her parents essentially made her an anchoress for the next ten years by keeping her in a room off the family's chapel, where she was seen only by a priest and a servant.

When Margaret was sixteen, her parents took her to nearby Città di Castello; a lay monk known for his holiness had recently died there, and it was thought that Margaret might experience a miraculous cure. When that didn't happen, her parents abandoned her.

The townspeople pitied her and began taking care of her. Margaret was then taken in by a monastery, as it was thought to be a good fit with her piety and self-deprivation. However, Margaret's zeal was too much for the nuns, and so she was turned out again. Finally, she found a loving home with a couple who accepted her as she was. She spent the rest of her short life as a Third Order Dominican, attending daily Mass, praying, and helping children learn about their faith.

Those who looked at Margaret with human eyes saw someone unworthy of life, someone whose trials may have been the work of the devil. But those who saw her as Jesus did saw a beautiful soul, full of love for God despite or perhaps because of the burdens she carried. They learned that every life, regardless of what the world says, is precious, and that God's healing starts on the inside and isn't always visible.

A Deeper Dive

"Little did she think, when she left home, what mercy was in store for her. Had she stayed in the house, or gone to see her friends, or been anywhere but where she was, she would have missed it all. So may we always, when in the way of duty, expect a blessing."
W. WALTERS[6]

Unforgettable You

CONTEMPLATION

Think about or discuss:

- What do you think happened to the woman who was healed of her disability? What might her life have been like five or ten years after the day of her healing?
- Why did Jesus call the woman "a daughter of Abraham"? What was the significance to the synagogue leader?
- Consider a time when you have judged or criticized another's good fortune rather than celebrating it. What can you learn from Jesus' words to the synagogue leader?

ACTION

Try walking bent at the waist without raising your head for sixty seconds. Note how slowly and tentatively you walk. Journal about this experience or about a time in your life when you couldn't raise your head emotionally or spiritually and what changed that experience.

PRAYER

Jesus, I thank you for the times
I was unaware of the weight
of my burdens until you lifted them
from me. May I do the same
for others in your name where
I can, feeding the hungry,
clothing the naked,
and visiting the prisoner.
Amen.

4

The Woman Whose Daughter Had an Unclean Spirit

A PLACE IN THE HOUSEHOLD

Jesus left that place and went away to the district of Tyre and Sidon. Just then a Canaanite woman from that region came out and started shouting, "Have mercy on me, Lord, Son of David; my daughter is tormented by a demon." But he did not answer her at all. And his disciples came and urged him, saying, "Send her away, for she keeps shouting after us." He answered, "I was sent only to the lost sheep of the house of Israel." But she came and knelt before him, saying, "Lord, help me." He answered, "It is not fair to take the children's food and throw it to the dogs." She said, "Yes, Lord, yet even the dogs eat the crumbs that fall from their masters' table." Then Jesus answered her, "Woman, great is your faith! Let it be done for you as you wish." And her daughter was healed from that moment. ◆ **MATTHEW 15:21–28**

Her Story

He belonged to the Jews, and she was a gentile. Still, she'd heard of his wonderful healings. Surely, he could help. She had faith.

The Canaanite woman (or Syrophoenician, according to the version in Mark's Gospel) likely was a widow since there's no mention of a husband. Mark uses "little" to describe the daughter. We don't know what the daughter's demonic possession looked like: possibly seizures, blindness, or another physical condition; possibly illness; possibly a huge change in mental or emotional health. The little girl may have been all the family the woman had. It had to cut at her heart and soul to see her daughter suffering and to be able to do nothing to relieve her misery.

Cross-References

JAMES 1:2–4
James counsels endurance and joy in times of faith testing

PHILIPPIANS 1:6
Paul assures the Philippians of God's faithfulness

LUKE 18:1–8
Parable of the widow and the unjust judge

Jesus and the disciples have traveled about thirty-five miles to the district of Tyre and Sidon after an intense time at Gennesaret on the Sea of Galilee's western shore. The disciples have witnessed the miracle of the loaves and fish, and Jesus has walked on water (so has Peter, briefly). Jesus has healed the sick and parried with the Pharisees and scribes about defilement. It comes from within, not from eating with unwashed hands, he says.

The crowds don't follow them northwest. It should be a bit of a respite for everyone. At least, until the woman comes on the scene, shouting for Jesus' help, falling at his feet, and generally annoying the disciples.

Have mercy, she says. My daughter is tormented.

Jesus knows he can cast out the demon. But she's a gentile, not a Jew. Up to now, he has focused his work on fulfilling the words of the Jewish prophets. Does she understand at all the enormity of his ministry, or is he just the latest provider of possible cures to her?

At first, he doesn't answer her. When the disciples urge him to send her away, he tests her, and it comes out hard to our modern ears:

"I was sent only to the lost souls of the house of Israel," he says.

She kneels and begs for help. His reply sounds even harsher this time: "It is not fair to take the children's food and throw it to the dogs."

Yes, Jesus seems to be equating her poor tormented daughter with a canine.

The woman understands that this is not rudeness, but a challenge. She does not take offense or hurl back an insult. Humbly, she presents him with a metaphor: Even the dogs eat crumbs that fall from the table. A crumb of grace will be just fine. And for a third time, she calls him "Lord."

Jesus says the words the woman most wanted to hear: what she wants will be done. She returns home to find her daughter healed.

WHAT HAPPENED TO THE WOMAN?

She must have been overjoyed when she saw that her daughter was healed. Did she regret not having stopped to thank Jesus profusely? Neither gospel shows any sign of that.

Having shown Jesus her great faith, perhaps she told the townspeople about the miracle—and about the mercy Jesus had extended to a gentile woman. Or is it possible that daily life intervened at some point, and her daughter's healing became an amazing story instead of a testimony of grace?

WHAT WE CAN LEARN FROM THE WOMAN

There's much to unpack about this woman. Let's start with the differences between Matthew's account and Mark's (Mark 7:24–30). They are subtle, but worth examining.

Matthew tells the story from a viewpoint he believes will resonate with his audience of Jews of the day who accepted the Old Testament prophecies. His aim was to show his peers through his accounts of Jesus' ministry that Jesus was the promised messiah. It is significant that according to Matthew, the Canaanite woman in her first plea calls Jesus "Lord, Son of David"; she acknowledges an understanding of his mission to date and that she is an outsider.

Matthew refers to her as a Canaanite woman, which likely indicates where she lives. Mark calls her a Syrophoenician, which may relate to her nationality or birthplace. They do not necessarily conflict; both gospel writers' intent is to make it clear that this woman most certainly is not an Israelite and does not practice the Jewish faith.

The woman is a little more desperate in Mark's account, actually entering a private house, presumably a Jewish family's residence. She begs for her daughter to be freed of the demon rather than asking Jesus to help the woman herself. The woman never calls Jesus "Lord"; she refers to him as "Sir" in the only words we hear directly from her in the New Revised Standard Version Updated Edition of the Bible. (A footnote says that earlier biblical accounts use "Lord" in this instance, or simply "Yes.") Mark says she finds out about the healing when she gets home; Matthew says the daughter was healed upon Jesus' words.

For me, the most important difference in the details is that in Matthew, the woman asks for help for herself—"Have mercy on me"—rather than for her daughter. We'll come back to that in a bit. But scholars seem to have always agreed that this is the same incident. And those of us in the pews have always struggled with Jesus' tone.

Jesus, in essence, tells the woman no—that his ministry is with the Israelites, not with the gentiles, and most certainly not with their historical enemies, the Canaanites. The woman accepts this. Rather than getting angry or defensive, her answer is, that is true. But I'm still part of the household, even if I rank only as high as the dogs. Even the dogs get fed.

Even the dogs get fed.

Consider the humility and the faith it took for the woman to say that. Like the woman at the well, she is challenging Jesus. But this challenge is different.

She acknowledged her perceived unworthiness—a gentile, and a woman at that. We all know what unworthiness looks like. We all know those times when we think our sin is too grave, our anger at God over a situation so deep that we know, just know, we can't or won't be forgiven. So, we try other remedies—food, alcohol, work, any other distraction—because we cannot and will not believe God still wants us.

And we are wrong, as the Canaanite woman knew. God does want us, and God's mercy is there for the asking.

It is hard to fathom that there was not good motivation behind Jesus' atypically less than loving, comforting words to someone who so respectfully asked for his help. Maybe he was illumining for the disciples that yes, he was the Messiah and, unlike in previous situations, his grace would extend far beyond the Jews, and his mission was larger than he had instructed them at their commissioning ("Do not take a road leading to gentiles, and do not enter a Samaritan town, but go rather to the lost sheep of the house of Israel" [Matthew 10:5–6]). Maybe that was the whole purpose behind that trip to Tyre and Sidon, for no other preaching or healing is recorded there. Or maybe Jesus learned something from the Canaanite woman that day.

In Matthew's Gospel, after this encounter, the group walks by the Sea of Galilee and goes up a mountain, where a "great crowd" was cured. Jesus then tells the disciples he has compassion for the crowd, which is surely starving. "I do not want to send them away hungry, for they might faint on the way" (Matthew 15:32).

One of the most public miracles in Jesus' ministry ensues: thousands of men, women, and children are fed by seven loaves of bread and a few small fish. Perhaps the Canaanite woman's refusal to go away hungry that day illumined for the human Jesus the enormity of his Divine mission. Perhaps it fed him.

A Story
A Place in the Household

I learned a great deal about the lie of unworthiness on my forty-ninth birthday. My roommate, a fellow teacher at a Christian writers' conference, was up with the sunrise around 5 AM As she exited to take a shower, my phone rang. The man I was seeing—not my estranged husband—called to wish me happy birthday. I ended the call unceremoniously when my roomie came out of the bathroom.

I was a fraud: a total fraud. Besides being an adulteress, I was a financial deadbeat. As I mentioned in chapter 1, I was repaying more than $100,000 in credit card debt that my estranged husband had racked up in my name, and in a good week I had fifty dollars to spend beyond rent and utilities. I had no business teaching at a Christian writers' conference. I hadn't been churched since I was fifteen. God had no interest in me. I knew that as sure as I knew my own name, so there was no point in trying to reach the Almighty. I shivered to think what my roommate, a well-published evangelical Christian, would do or say if she knew the truth about me.

I was supposed to be on a business conference call in the evening, but my cell phone wasn't working. My guess was that my husband hadn't paid the bill. Roomie was quick to offer the use of her cell phone, but I declined. I hated the idea of being beholden in any way to such a perfect Christian.

So, I walked a mile to the nearest service station pay phone. The conference call went on for an hour. The station driveway bell signal clanged almost constantly, making it impossible to hear most of the call, other than the very end, when the other participants sang "Happy Birthday" to me.

Some happy birthday, I muttered as I walked back as the sun was setting at 9 PM. I hoped my roomie was asleep or out doing good works.

But she was waiting up. She was worried about me.

The words tumbled out of my mouth before I could stop them: I need you to pray over me, right now, for I am lost and undeserving and I can't pray for myself because God wouldn't listen anyway. But please pray over me.

She did, without questions and without hesitation.

We talked a little afterward, then went to bed. It was the most peaceful sleep I'd had in a long time. If she thought I was worth a prayer, maybe I was. And maybe I wasn't of as little interest to God as I thought. Maybe I was still part of the household.

A Deeper Dive

"This is what this woman teaches us, this wonderful mother: the courage to bring our own painful story before God, before Jesus, to touch God's tenderness, Jesus' tenderness. Let's try this story, this prayer: let each one of us think of his or her own story. There are always ugly things in a story, always. Let us go to Jesus, knock on Jesus' heart and say to Him: 'Lord, if you will it, you can heal me!'"

POPE FRANCIS, AUGUST 16, 2020[7]

Finding Our Place:
Saint Magdalena of Canossa (1774–1835)

Magdalena, founder of the Canossian Daughters of Charity, provides an example of struggling to find our place—and finding it, with the Lord's help.

While Magdalena's faith was strong, at times it had to have seemed that the Lord's attention was elsewhere. For the first thirty or so years of her life, challenges and upheaval were common. The third child born into wealthy Italian family, she was just five years old when her father died. Her mother remarried two years later and abandoned Magdalena and her siblings. An uncle became their guardian; he employed a stern governess with whom the children had a difficult relationship.

At fifteen, Magdalena was recovering from a serious illness when she decided God was calling her to be a nun. When she was seventeen, she entered a Carmelite convent but stayed only ten months. Soon after, she tried a second religious community but left after just three days.

Her desire to be a nun was seemingly not in alignment with God's plan for her; Magdalena returned home to Verona to manage her family's sizable estate. This was no small undertaking, given their status; in June 1805, shortly after his coronation as king of Italy, Napoleon came to Canossa Palace.

By that time, Magdalena was beginning to better understand the ministry to which the Lord was calling her. She was helping at-risk young women by renting homes for them in Verona, even housing some at the palace, and setting up a school. In fact, Magdalena was staying at one of those homes when Napoleon visited.

When she shared with her family her desire to form a community of religious women to minister to the poor, their initial reaction was less than supportive. That was understandable; in addition to running the estate and her outside ministries (which relatives felt were inappropriate for a woman of her class), Magdalena was also responsible for an uncle's medical care and the education of a nephew.

Eventually, Magdalena's humble persistence prevailed, and the family relented. Shortly after her thirty-fourth birthday, she left Canossa Palace behind and, with companions, formed what we know today as the Canossian Daughters of Charity, Servants of the Poor. The community spread rapidly in Italy, and its rule was formally approved in 1828. The Canossians today are a community of more than two thousand sisters in North and South America, Asia, Africa, Europe, and Australia. "Above all, make Jesus known," one of Magdalena's sayings, remains a challenge for all the community members.

About fifty years after Magdalena's death, an Italian vice-consul left his young daughter and her enslaved nanny in the care of the Canossians in Venice when he and his wife went to Sudan on business. It was with this community that Saint Josephine Bakhita (1869–1947), who as a child had been kidnapped by slave traders in Sudan, found freedom and Christ and inspired the world with her charism of forgiveness.

Unforgettable You

CONTEMPLATION

Think about or discuss:

- What do you think happened to the woman who pleaded with Jesus? What might her life have been like five or ten years after this day?
- How do you frame your prayer requests? For example, do you pray, "God, heal my spouse," or do you pray, "God, help me to provide comfort and support to my spouse"?
- What is the difference between the humble persistence shown by the woman whose daughter had an unclean spirit and Magdalena of Canossa… the pride and stubbornness in staying on a path that the Lord may not desire?

ACTION

Create a scrapbook page or journal entry about a time when you did the Lord's bidding and other people questioned your judgment. Perhaps it had to do with your spouse or your children or a job situation.

PRAYER

Jesus, your heart was touched by the Canaanite woman's humility and faith. May I remember that those are the gifts that mean the most to you and offer them unstintingly. Amen.

5

The Woman Healed by a Touch

OUTER TRAPPINGS, INNER POWER

Then suddenly a woman who had been suffering from a flow of blood for twelve years came up behind him and touched the fringe of his cloak, for she was saying to herself, "If I only touch his cloak, I will be made well." Jesus turned, and seeing her he said, "Take heart, daughter; your faith has made you well." And the woman was made well from that moment. ◆ **MATTHEW 9:20–22**

Her Story

She is desperate.

The flow of blood had begun twelve years earlier, and no one has been able to help her. She is unclean according to the law, and the continuing flow keeps her from being purified. She is not supposed to touch anyone, not even her family, if she has one. Nor could she prepare their meals. If she was married, this would have given her husband grounds to divorce her. She can't even go inside the temple.

She has heard of this Jesus and all his healings. If he could heal people who were blind, deaf, and possessed, maybe there is hope for her.

The woman hears the hubbub when Jesus returns with his disciples; she slips into the crowd, disguised in some way. Jairus, a Capernaum synagogue leader,

Cross-References

LUKE 8:43–48
and **MARK 5:25–34**
The woman is healed simply by touching Jesus

NUMBERS 15:37–40
God tells Moses to have the Israelites make fringes on the corners of their garments as a reminder of the commandments

MATTHEW 23:5
Jesus denounces the scribes and Pharisees for their pride and hypocrisy

kneels before Jesus and begs him to heal his dying or dead twelve-year-old daughter.

When Jesus agrees and begins to follow Jairus, the woman sees her opportunity. If she can just touch his clothes, she knows she will be healed. It's crowded; any number of people are jostling him, and so, down on her knees, crawling, she gets near him and touches his cloak and prepares to make her exit.

But Jesus stops and turns. He sees her. Her heart skips a beat. Will he call out her uncleanliness in front of all these people? Will they lay hands upon her for her crime?

But no. He looks her in the eyes and says, "Take heart, daughter; your faith has made you well."

She can feel that the bleeding has stopped in that very moment. She'd like to thank Jesus, to kiss his feet, but he and the crowd have already moved on.

WHAT HAPPENED TO THE WOMAN?

The Eastern Orthodox Church names the healed woman Veronica and considers her a saint. (She is not the same person as the Roman Catholic Church's Saint Veronica, who according to tradition offered her veil to Jesus to wipe his face on the way to the crucifixion.) The Eastern Orthodox tradition is that Veronica remained a follower of Christ and led a holy life. In the Roman Catholic tradition, the healed woman is not named.

What happened to the woman in the immediate aftermath of her healing? Did those in her community who had been isolated from her welcome her with open arms? Did she resume participation at the temple? Did she continue to follow Jesus?

Or did she remain set apart, with people disbelieving and distrusting her miraculous cure?

WHAT WE CAN LEARN FROM THE WOMAN

Sight, hearing, touch, taste, smell. Our Catholic faith, lived at its deepest, is fed by all five senses.

Touch may be the most difficult for non-Catholics to understand. Many of us touch the Eucharist, albeit momentarily, during Mass. The things we touch—holy water, rosary beads, holy cards, Passion Sunday palms, reliquaries—serve as reminders of the sacraments we have received and of how the lives of our beloved saints can inspire us. We don't worship sacramentals and relics; we worship God, and God alone. But the things we touch resonate deeply in our souls.

This was not the worldview of the woman with the flow of blood. As a Jew, she was aware of the Lord's order to Moses: "Speak to the Israelites, and tell them to make fringes on the corners of their garments throughout their generations and to put a blue cord on the fringe at each corner. You have the fringe so that, when you see it, you will remember all the commandments of the LORD and do them and not follow the lust of your own heart and your own eyes" (Numbers 15:37–39). The fringes, or *tzitzit* in Hebrew, still are worn today. They are outward signs of a spiritual leader.

The woman had a transactional hope: if she touched the cloak, she could be healed. That was all that would need to happen. And indeed, both Luke's and Mark's accounts say she was healed by that touch, though things get less anonymous than she had hoped for when Jesus feels the power leave him and asks who touched him.

For me, Matthew's version speaks the most profoundly. She touches the cloak, all right, but it is not until Jesus speaks the words—"Take heart, daughter; your faith has made you well"—that she is healed.

Remember, Matthew's desired audience was Jewish Christians. Later (Matthew 23:5), Jesus warns of the scribes' and Pharisees' hypocrisy, that they "make their phylacteries [cases containing Torah texts] broad and their fringes long" as symbols of their desire for admiration rather than easing the burdens of the people.

The woman didn't want to bother Jesus. Unlike, for example, the woman whose daughter was possessed by a demon, she didn't seek his attention by calling out to him. The less attention she drew from anyone that day, the better, she thought; that way, no one would recognize her and call her out for disobeying the law. In fact, she probably was grateful for all the commotion going on with Jairus' plea for help with his daughter. The woman thought it would make her touch go unnoticed. She had hope of healing, but faith in Jesus? Hard to tell.

However, Jesus is not a magician. If he were, he would have cured everyone he encountered. That wasn't his purpose. He came to redeem us and offer us the hope of eternal life in heaven. Our encounters with him that bear the most fruit are not transactional; they are transformational. They require more than a single touch. They require a friendship, a relationship.

Second, the woman's story teaches us that we should not be quiet about what Jesus does in our lives. She was grateful, of course, but quite possibly the last thing she wanted was attention drawn to how she was healed.

Jesus gave her the potential to become an evangelist that day. The crowd may not have recognized her in her disguise, but they knew Jesus had done something important. It wasn't about her individually; it was about his grace.

It's a sometimes difficult balance, glorifying God and all the Almighty has done versus bragging about our good fortune. But when we frame it as gratitude, we invite others to get to know the Lord. Sharing our struggles and our victories helps bring people to Christ. Remaining silent about his grace and goodness does not.

A Story
Healing

If those words make you itchy—friendship and relationship with Jesus—I understand. They're hard for me too; after all, Jesus is the only begotten Son of God. It's challenging for me to think that he has the time or interest to hear about the difficulty I had in writing some parts of this book or why I wish I were less of a people pleaser.

But in my more faith-filled moments, when I can turn things around and ask him for help with writing or to show me his priorities for me, I believe he does have both the time and the interest, because he loves me and desires to help me do God's will. And Jesus always comes through—maybe not in the way I wanted or expected, but he always comes through.

Jesus can do the things, and often he does, without us desiring or expecting any more from him or giving him much back. But we can have more than the things if we are willing to commit and believe.

A Deeper Dive

"She wanted health; she did not care about the Healer. She thought much of the blessing in itself, little or nothing of the blessing as a sign of his love. She would have been quite contented to have had nothing more to do with Christ if she could only have gone away cured. She felt but little glow of gratitude to him whom she thought of as unconscious of the good which she had stolen from him. All this is a parallel to what occurs in the early stages of many a Christian life."
ALEXANDER MACLAREN (1826–1910), SCOTTISH BAPTIST MINISTER[8]

This story may sound silly, but it is true and it has helped me a great deal. A few years back, my sister and I bought a condo two blocks from the apartment building where we'd lived for ten years. We had the place inspected, we had the contract reviewed, and everything was in order. Until after we closed on the purchase and I tried to drive my Honda Accord into the assigned condo parking lot. It wouldn't fit. Nor would a friend's Ford Fiesta. We had two weeks left on the apartment lease and the parking spot there.

My sister left for an international business trip the next day, so I was on my own: calling the zoning board, calling our real estate agent, talking to the condo manager. I got the same answer from everyone: when the condo was built, the county didn't require all such spaces to be a standard size, and the building's lot was grandfathered by the regulations of that time. I had two choices: pay hundreds of dollars a month at a nearby commercial lot or sell the car.

I complained to friends, I cried, I got angry. I did everything other than take the situation to prayer. Then, with three days left, I was driving home from speaking to some folks about the women saints. About three miles from home, I finally prayed: Lord, I am troubled beyond words. Help! Tell me what to do.

And he did. He said, in what to me was an audible voice, "Don't sell the car."

Truly, there was great calm then. I went to the apartment building that night and left the manager a note asking if I could continue to park there for a while. She said yes, for less than ten percent of what the commercial garages were charging. Two years later, after my sister and I had realized by this and other experiences that condo ownership wasn't for us, the apartment building manager made our return to happy rentership a breeze.

Now, you might roll your eyes and say, "Really, Melanie, you wasted the Lord's time on *that*?" Yes—yes, I did. And I have told that story to more people, Christian and otherwise, than I complained to in the two weeks I tried to handle the car problem on my own. They may not believe me. *You* may not believe me. But to me, it is a witness of healing.

Abandoning Outer Trappings: *Saint Ursula Ledóchowska (1865–1939)*

When you think of modern-day women saints associated with Poland, Faustina probably comes to mind almost immediately. Next, you might think of Teresa Benedicta of the Cross (Edith

Stein), who was born in what is now Poland and died with her sister at Auschwitz.

Julia Maria Ledóchowska was a generation older than those two beloved women, and you likely haven't heard of her. Poland didn't exist when she was born in 1865; while her father was a member of Polish nobility, she was born at the family estate in Austria. It was not until she was seventeen that the family moved permanently to her father's homeland. By that time, Julia had determined that she had a vocation as an Ursuline nun; she became a novice in Kraków when she was twenty-one. Taking the name Maria Ursula of Jesus, she had a relatively quiet life for the next twenty years in convent leadership and in establishing a residence for female college students.

Impressed by her work, Pope Pius X directed her in 1907 to undertake similar work in Saint Petersburg. As the Russian political climate grew more and more difficult, she and her sisters abandoned their habits, wearing gray clothing to indicate their evangelization. It is difficult to imagine the challenge of being a woman religious, identifiable by your habit for twenty or so years, only to lose that instant visible sign of your vocation. However, the sisters pressed on with their work.

Russia expelled the community in 1914 with the dawning of World War I; Ursula and then others relocated to Scandinavia, where they were involved in war refugee relief efforts and set up girls' schools. Ursula also was known as an excellent orator and a tireless advocate for Polish independence, frequently speaking on Polish history and culture throughout the region.

Poland became an independent nation again at the end of the war, and Ursula and her sisters returned to the country in 1920. Her convent was re-formed into the Ursulines of the Agonizing

Heart of Jesus, which continues to aid poor and uneducated people in fourteen countries.

Ursula's example reminds us that, like Jesus and the hem of his garment and the clergy's clerical clothing, our outward trappings can signal our availability to people in spiritual need. Ultimately, though, our hearts, souls, eyes, ears, and tongues are our best ways to invite people to get to know Jesus and trust in his touch.

Unforgettable You

CONTENTMPLATION

Think about or discuss:

- What do you think happened to the woman with the flow of blood? What might her life have been like five or ten years after this day?
- What signs of your faith do you show to the world, inviting others to get to know Jesus through you?
- Where are you bleeding spiritually? What is keeping you from taking it to Jesus?

ACTION

Make a list or collage showing the ways your faith was strengthened this week by all five senses.

PRAYER

Jesus, help me to believe
that you always have time for me—
and that I always have time
for you. Amen.

6

The Woman Caught in Adultery

UNDESERVED MERCY

Early in the morning he came again to the temple. All the people came to him, and he sat down and began to teach them. The scribes and the Pharisees brought a woman who had been caught in adultery, and, making her stand before all of them, they said to him, "Teacher, this woman was caught in the very act of committing adultery. Now in the law Moses commanded us to stone such women. Now what do you say?" They said this to test him, so that they might have some charge to bring against him. Jesus bent down and wrote with his finger on the ground. When they kept on questioning him, he straightened up and said to them, "Let anyone among you who is without sin be the first to throw a stone at her." And once again he bent down and wrote on the ground. When they heard it, they went away, one by one, beginning with the elders, and Jesus was left alone with the woman standing before him. Jesus straightened up and said to her, "Woman, where are they? Has no one condemned you?" She said, "No one, sir." And Jesus said, "Neither do I condemn you. Go your way, and from now on do not sin again." ◆ **JOHN 8:2–11**

Cross-References

JEREMIAH 33:8
The Lord's promise of forgiveness and cleansing for Israel and Juda

SIRACH 5:5–7
A reminder that penance should not be undertaken lightly

EPHESIANS 4:32
Paul counsels the Ephesians to forgive each other as Christ forgives them

Her Story

She knows what is coming.

The law was quite clear: a betrothed virgin or a wife who was found to be having sex with another man was to be put to death. If she hadn't cried out for help, it didn't matter if the act had been against her will within the city. It didn't matter if she was in a loveless, abusive marriage and had succumbed once to the temptation presented by someone who seemed kind and compassionate. It didn't matter whether the accusation was true, as long as two people said it had happened. And it didn't even matter if she was hired to play a part to entrap Jesus; if so, those who hired her had tricked her.

She is going to die.

She knows it will be a slow, painful death. She will be secured in some way—tied to a tree or pillar, maybe, or possibly partially buried in a pit—then be struck by stones tossed by the community, beginning with the witnesses. It might take thirty minutes or more.

Is she shaking, crying, trying to cover her body with her hands and hair, begging for mercy? Or does she hold her head high, knowing the circumstances under which the offense had occurred—and perhaps knowing the offenses of those to her right and her left—and saying nothing? Does she wonder why she hadn't been taken to the civil authorities, since religious leaders at that time did not have the power to order an execution? And where is the man involved—escaped? Already dead? Awaiting his own grisly end? We don't know.

What we do know is that this woman has been, the scribes and Pharisees say, "caught in the very act." What will Jesus have to say about that?

Here's how Saint John Paul II put Jesus' position in an April 1, 2001, homily: "If he absolves the woman caught in flagrant adultery, it will be said that he has transgressed the precepts of Moses; if he condemns her, it will be said that he is inconsistent with his message of mercy towards sinners."[1]

Jesus does neither. Stooping down, he uses his finger to write on the ground. (It may not have been lost on some in the crowd that the stone tablets Moses brought down from Mount Sinai had been "written with the finger of God" [Exodus 31:18].) Pressed for an answer, Jesus stands and calls on the sinless to throw stones first, then he resumes writing. Eventually, everyone leaves except the woman. She doesn't walk, run, or skip away. She doesn't fall at his feet, offering gratitude, or confess. She's just there. Maybe she feels safer there than anyplace else she can think of.

Rhetorically, Jesus asks if any of her accusers remain. No, she says. And it is there that we begin to understand the gift of God's mercy—and the obligation we incur in accepting it:

"Neither do I condemn you. Go your way, and from now on do not sin again" (John 8:11).

WHAT HAPPENED TO THE WOMAN?

Some think the woman caught in adultery was Mary Magdalene and that the woman may have been possessed by demons. There is no consensus among scholars about this, and the story of Mary Magdalene being a prostitute has been debunked.[2]

If she wasn't Mary Magdalene and she wasn't hired and then duped by the scribes and Pharisees, this day may have changed her life. Perhaps this message of forgiveness prompted her to reassess her actions, to end the relationship with the other man, to attempt to repair things with her husband.

But the woman shares no contrition in this passage from John. Perhaps she was too shocked at her rescue to offer gratitude, or maybe she was too angry at what had happened before she was brought to Jesus.

Perhaps she mended her ways and became one of Jesus' followers.

Or maybe she went back into town and was a pariah.

WHAT WE CAN LEARN FROM THE WOMAN

Think about or discuss: What was it that Jesus wrote in the sand both times? What about the other person—we will assume it was a man—involved in the adultery, and why wasn't he dragged before Jesus too? Why didn't the woman run away as soon as her accusers had dispersed?

Good questions, and as you'll see later in the discussion section, I hope some of them will prompt thoughtful internal or group conversation. But in focusing on the particulars, we lose sight of the larger message. We forget, as Jesus told the Pharisees when they criticized his disciples for plucking grain on the Sabbath, that something greater than the temple is here.

You see, to her accusers the woman was a tool, not a human being. They were using her to trap Jesus. That was what was important to them, not her crime.

This is further borne out by their lack of compassion. She's dragged, likely at least half naked, into the temple and forced to stand. Her accusers have no respect for her intrinsic human dignity, nor do the ogling onlookers.

But God's justice is always trumped by God's love, and the thumb of mercy is on the scale. Jesus makes the story about her as a person and the potential for her redemption.

We don't know the woman's full story any more than we know the full story of the latest mass murderer or those of the priest whose homilies are always interminably long or the neighbors who don't cut their grass as often as we'd like.

And we don't need to.

People sometimes get off scot-free: in the workplace, in marriages, in the world. Typically, we are not called to be their judge, jury, or executioner. Sometimes, the Lord places it on our heart to provide gentle, loving correction and speak truth—but not to judge or condemn.

Jesus is silent when the noisy group enters the area where he is preaching; he lets the scene unfold. Then he straightens up and looks them in the eye. An uncomfortable silence falls over the group. Then Jesus speaks. We can imagine his tone being calm but authoritative. His words so shame them and their self-righteousness and trickery that they slink out quietly one by one, starting with the elders.

Only then does Jesus address the woman, and it is then that he shares another important lesson. She does not confess, even though her sin of adultery is apparent. His counsel: "From now on do not sin again."

Like the woman—and, indeed, like the Pharisees in this story—our sin may be apparent. The Lord will forgive any sin and make us clean. But for that to happen, we must acknowledge our wrongdoing and repent. Grace and mercy are free; Jesus bought them for us with his life. If we accept them without redirecting ourselves to the right path, they can be lost.

A Story
Mercy or the Lack Thereof

When I was younger, I knew right from wrong—for everyone. I liked to credit that to being the eldest daughter of an eldest daughter of an eldest daughter and to having an arrogant, narcissistic father. I knew the right way to put toilet paper on a holder, to study for a test, to fold towels, to write a newspaper article, and I was not shy about sharing those certainties.

In short, it was exhausting to be around me. It was exhausting to *be* me, the person someone once nicknamed "Supercop of the World."

The staff at my college newspaper was a tight-knit bunch—we hung out at the office together, went to classes (occasionally) together, and partied (often) together. Some also became romantically involved, and one couple is still going strong more than forty years later.

This story is not about them. It's about a couple who were not married. In fact, one of them was married to someone else and had a child. Yet, they were quite public about their romance. That shocked and appalled me. And besides gossiping about it with a few other staffers, I knew I had to do something about it.

I became a Pharisee.

At the time, personal ads in newspapers, including ours, were well-read items. So, a friend and I put an ad in the personals, reversing the lovebirds' initials and noting that "The Committee" knew about their affair. Then we sat back to watch the show.

No one ever called us out on it, but the romance ended, at least publicly. The meandering staffer's spouse and child didn't come into the office anymore. There was a noticeable chill in the newsroom. I stepped back from a leadership role the following semester to focus on my studies so I could graduate at the end of the term.

The older I got, the more judgment errors of my own I made. They and God's grace in leading me to a right path taught me that good friends speak truth to you directly, in a loving way, when you go astray. They don't hide behind anonymity any more than God does.

For a while, I considered sending apologies to the parties—they're easy to find, and the married couple stayed married—but decided against it. I reasoned that the apologies could open old wounds and would be about me, not about them. Eventually, I forgave myself—but I still think of this incident when I am tempted to resume my supercop behavior.

A dear friend (who went to college four states and nearly nine hundred miles away) and I were talking about regrets a few years ago. She has crossed paths professionally with one of the adulterers. When she said that the person was not deserving of my thoughts or contrition, I told her that didn't matter. These days, I work at letting God do the judging. My role is to love and to work on making my own behavior more pleasing to the Lord.

A Deeper Dive

"The Scribes have a zeal for public welfare and so has Christ. In their case coarse sin mixed with cruel anger unite to destroy a poor sinner; in his infinite purity mixed with tenderest love unite to destroy sin and save the sinner. He does not pardon because she has not yet repented; but, declining to condemn her, he bids her 'go and sin no more.'"
R. GLOVER[9]

Accepting Undeserved Mercy: *Saint Mary of Egypt (c. 344–c. 421)*

It does not appear that Mary of Egypt was an adulteress. Nor was she a sex worker in the traditional sense. Some accounts—not the one she gave to a monk shortly before her death—posit that she was sexually abused as a young church cantor or was a nun who ran away from the convent because someone possessed by a demon was pursuing her.

According to Mary, by way of the monk we know as Zosimas of Palestine, she left home at age twelve for Alexandria and proceeded to engage in a life of debauchery. Her livelihood primarily came from begging and spinning flax; while she had many sexual partners, she often refused their payment.

When she was nearing thirty, Mary encountered a group of pilgrims headed for Jerusalem. She saw this as an opportunity for new escapades and talked her way into joining them.

But upon her arrival at the Church of the Holy Sepulchre, she was stopped from entering by a presence she could not see. Again and again, she tried. Each time, she was unsuccessful. She realized that this was because of her many sins. Mary turned to an icon of the Blessed Virgin located outside the church and bared her soul in prayer. She then was able to enter the church, where she heard a voice say that she would find peace if she crossed the Jordan River. Chastened and reborn, she made a full confession at a nearby monastery, then went into the desert.

It was there that Zosimas encountered her, decades later, almost unrecognizable as a human being. She shared her story, including her continual battle with temptation despite living as a hermit. She asked the monk to return to the same spot the following year on Holy Thursday and to bring the Eucharist. He did so, and she asked him to return the following year as well. At that time, he found her dead body and a notation in the sand that she had died the same day he had left.

Mary was divinely led to Jerusalem; there is no doubt of that, nor is there any doubt that she confessed her sins fully and intentionally. But engaging God in the fight allowed her and the Almighty to emerge victorious and allowed her to lie down and die in peace.

Unforgettable You

CONTENTION

Think about or discuss:

- What do you think happened to the woman caught in adultery? What might her life have been like five or ten years after this day?
- What do you think Jesus wrote on the ground?
- Why didn't the woman ask for forgiveness, and why did Jesus give it to her without her asking?

ACTION

Go to confession. In your examen, pay particular attention to the times you have judged rather than leaving it to God.

PRAYER

Jesus, I see myself in the Pharisees in the story of the woman caught in adultery. Help me to drop the stones in my heart and hands and not judge people. When you call me to speak truth on your behalf, guide my words that I may provide gentle, loving correction. Amen.

7

The Woman with the Alabaster Jar

SEEING WITH CHRIST'S EYES

One of the Pharisees asked Jesus to eat with him, and when he went into the Pharisee's house he reclined to dine. And a woman in the city who was a sinner, having learned that he was eating in the Pharisee's house, brought an alabaster jar of ointment. She stood behind him at his feet, weeping, and began to bathe his feet with her tears and to dry them with her hair, kissing his feet and anointing them with the ointment. Now when the Pharisee who had invited him saw it, he said to himself, "If this man were a prophet, he would have known who and what kind of woman this is who is touching him, that she is a sinner." Jesus spoke up and said to him, "Simon, I have something to say to you." "Teacher," he replied, "speak." "A certain moneylender had two debtors; one owed five hundred denarii, and the other fifty. When they could not pay, he canceled the debts for both of them. Now which of them will love him more?" Simon answered, "I suppose the one for whom he canceled the greater debt." And Jesus said to him, "You have judged rightly." Then turning toward the woman, he said to Simon, "Do you see this woman? I entered your house; you gave me no water for my feet, but she has bathed my feet with her tears and dried them with her hair. You gave me no kiss, but from the time I came in she has not stopped kissing my feet. You did not anoint my head with oil, but she has anointed my feet with ointment. Therefore, I tell you, her many sins have been forgiven; hence she has shown great love. But the one to whom little is forgiven loves little." Then he said to her, "Your sins are forgiven." But those who were at the table with him began to say among themselves, "Who is this who even forgives sins?" But he said to the woman, "Your faith has saved you; go in peace." ◆ **LUKE 7:36–50**

Cross-References

JOHN 12:1–8
Mary of Bethany is identified as the woman, and Judas as the challenger

MARK 14:3–9
Critics scold the woman

MATTHEW 26:6–13
The disciples are angry about the expense

Her Story

She was a sinner.

She knew that. Simon the Pharisee knew that. And she knew the Pharisee knew that. They had some history; she knew where he lived and how to get into the house where Jesus and the others would be eating. And while she was a sinner, he didn't consider her enough of a threat or unclean enough to have her thrown out when she entered. (Or maybe he thought her presence would add to the evening's entertainment.) She was counting on that, or she was willing to accept the risk.

The nature and gravity of her sin are not disclosed. Whatever it was, she decided it was time to start afresh. But to do this, she needed Jesus' forgiveness. So, she found the wherewithal to obtain a small alabaster jar and filled it with nard, a soothing ointment.

As per the custom, Jesus is lying down, propped up on one elbow, for the meal. The woman doesn't stand in front of him; perhaps she is too overwhelmed by his presence or too frightened of the others. She begins to cry and then, still behind him, falls to her knees. Her tears bathe his feet. She undoes her hair and uses it as a towel of sorts, then kisses his feet and breaks open the jar. She rubs the ointment into those feet, and the room fills with a woodsy, musky scent.

The woman hears the voices of Jesus and the Pharisee, but it is as if they are speaking another language. She puts every ounce of her attention into anointing his feet, confessing and asking for forgiveness with each rub.

Suddenly, she realizes he is now speaking to her: "Your sins are forgiven." She draws a deep breath. Can it be true? And he says: "Your faith has saved you; go in peace."

WHAT HAPPENED TO THE WOMAN?

Some scholars believe the penitent woman in Luke's account was Mary Magdalene, the first person to whom the resurrected Jesus revealed himself in John's Gospel. John's own account of this incident, however, identifies Mary of Bethany, the sister of Martha and Lazarus, as the woman who anointed Jesus' head with nard. Mark and Matthew provide no name for the woman.

Tradition holds that both Mary Magdalene and Mary of Bethany remained believers for the rest of their lives.

If the penitent woman is someone else, she seems to have experienced a true conversion. I'd like to think the faith and confidence and bravery she showed in entering the Pharisee's home that day and humbling herself in anointing Jesus' feet grew even stronger with time, and that she went on to fearlessly and tirelessly evangelize, regardless of what people thought or said about her. Did she become perfect? Highly unlikely; she was human. But she knew where to go to find forgiveness and start anew.

WHAT WE CAN LEARN FROM THE WOMAN

As noted above, Mark and Matthew provide no name for the woman, but their accounts otherwise are very similar to John's—a woman anoints Jesus, while others present grumble about the outrageous expense and say the funds should have gone to the poor. Jesus reminds them to value what they have in him.

A profound lesson, to be sure, but Luke's purpose is different. Unlike the other three gospel accounts, no one in Luke's narrative complains about the high cost of nard.

In Luke, Jesus is not at a friend's home but at a Pharisee's house in Capernaum. That shouldn't surprise us; Jesus dined with tax collectors and sinners, and he encouraged others to do the same, so why not a Pharisee?

The Pharisee, however, does not engage with Jesus like a valued guest. He doesn't welcome him in any way. He, in essence, treats Jesus like the evening's entertainment, a show pony to amuse the others. He doesn't even stop or question the penitent woman when she enters and starts weeping over Jesus' feet.

The Pharisee likely knew the woman and didn't regard her as dangerous. But the look on his face showed his displeasure—not with the woman, for she was who she was, but with Jesus. What was Jesus thinking, letting this sinner *touch* him?

To the Pharisee, the woman was one-dimensional: a sinner. He didn't know or care about the circumstances that led her to sin, and he certainly wasn't interested in the possibility of her becoming clean again. She wasn't of his gender or class, and that meant she was no one. Similarly, Jesus to him was one-dimensional: someone with whom to have interesting, challenging conversations, but not his equal in any way.

Jesus, on the other hand, immediately recognized a woman on the precipice of conversion. He knew she was confessing and doing penance by her very presence and with every tear, every drop of oil, every rub of his feet. When she broke the neck on that alabaster container, she also broke open her soul. And neither could ever be closed up again.

The Pharisee was unconcerned about the woman's past, and he certainly did not see a role for himself in helping her to navigate to a better tomorrow. Jesus knew but did not excuse her past. And he understood that the faith she showed in those faltering steps into the house, in getting on her knees, and in bathing and anointing him cost much more than any ointment. She had sinned large. Now, she was ready to love large as well.

Jesus believed the woman was repenting for her sins and was willing to take a chance on her sincerity. Think of the prodigal son: he never exactly says he's sorry for his dissolute behavior. He may just be hungry, but he knows the words to say to his father.

Maybe he meant them that day, or maybe he came to mean them in the days or weeks after his father's expansive welcome. That's the thing about continual conversion; we always have the opportunity to deepen our gratitude.

If we're the prodigal son's brother in the story, we know how hard it can be to accept someone's change without some skepticism. But we please Jesus when we set aside that skepticism—which may be evil's whisper—and err on the side of forgiveness and embrace.

A Story
Seeing with Christ's Eyes

The priest who successfully advocated for my annulment a few years back is a canon law expert. He was in the United States for a few years on a special assignment and now is back in his native Nigeria, where he is in a leadership role with the Dominicans.

Father Charles' first assignment after ordination was with a rural parish in Nigeria. A woman in the community practiced a form of witchcraft. People were convinced, he said, that the woman cast spells that ruined their crops, killed their animals, and worse. She was universally feared, and people were careful not to anger her.

One day, Father Charles was called to the woman's home. She was dying. She told him she was sorry for all the hurt she had inflicted and asked him to baptize her as a Catholic and to bury her in the church's cemetery. After listening some more and asking her questions, Father Charles was convinced her conversion was true. He baptized her, and she died not long afterward.

The community was aghast when Father Charles told them of this remarkable conversation. The woman had wounded his parishioners deeply over the years, and they saw this as yet another trick. They were sure she could not have truly repented. Ultimately, the bishop had to get involved; he agreed to the burial, based on Father Charles' testimony.

Had the woman's confession been real? I hope I would have had faith enough to support Father Charles and believe in the miracles that Christ's mercy can work in the worst of sinners. After all, it's what Jesus asks of us—and does for us.

A Deeper Dive

"We pass our hasty sentence upon thousands and tens of thousands of erring beings, not considering for a moment how many among them are devoured by an unspeakable remorse; how many are capable of sorrow, though they stave it off; [how] few, comparatively, are the hopeless children of perdition, lost in this world and the world to come."
CHURCH OF ENGLAND ARCHBISHOP WILLIAM THOMSON (1819–1880)[10]

Seeing with Christ's Eyes:
Saint Laura Montoya Upegui (Laura of St. Catherine of Siena) (1874–1949)

The Colombian towns of Jericó, where Laura was born, and Dabeiba, where she did most of her ministry, are less than 150 miles away from each other and today have similar populations. They are south and north, respectively, of Medellín. But in other ways, they are worlds apart.

Jericó's elevation is more than 6,200 feet. The town gets about 100 inches of rain each year, and the temperature is almost always in the low 70s during the day and mid-60s at night. By contrast, Dabeiba's elevation is less than 1,500 feet. It's in a rainforest, and annual precipitation is more than ten percent more than that of Jericó. Dabeiba also gets about ten degrees hotter during the day and doesn't cool down much at night.

In Laura's time, people in the mountains didn't know much about the Indigenous people who lived in the rainforest region. Non-familiarity has a way of breeding fear, contempt, and judgment. The rainforest residents were called "wild beasts" and regarded as barely human.

Even though she was from the mountains, Laura was used to being judged as an outsider. When she was two, her father died in a civil war. That left Laura, two siblings, and her mother all but destitute. Laura was sent to live with a less than loving grandmother, then to an orphanage managed by one of Laura's aunts, a nun.

When Laura was sixteen, her mother decided it was time for the girl to become a teacher to support the family financially. No matter that she had never had any formal education. Still, she thrived at teachers' school and enjoyed working with students, both on their academics and on their religious formation.

She wondered if she had a vocation as a Carmelite nun but determined that her vocation was to bring Jesus to those who did not know him. That vocation was cemented when, as a teacher, she received an assignment with Indigenous people.

Just before her fortieth birthday, Laura and four friends moved to Dabeiba as missionaries. Many people couldn't understand why they wanted to work with "those people"; the women might be injured, assaulted, or killed. But Laura knew they were created in God's image, just like her.

Laura spent most of the rest of her life in the rainforest, living as the Indigenous people and evangelizing. Today, the community is known as the Congregation of the Missionary Sisters of Immaculate Mary and St. Catherine of Siena. Today, the sisters continue in nineteen countries the work she began.

Unforgettable You

CONTEMPLATION

Think about or discuss:

- What do you think happened to the woman with the alabaster jar? What might her life have been like five or ten years after this encounter with Jesus?
- What alabaster jar is the Lord calling you to break open for him? Your pride? Your fear? Your shyness or some other perceived inadequacy?
- Is there someone you identify, from real-life experience or gossip, as a sinner to be avoided? Consider praying for that person or, if it is safe, spending some time with them in a public setting.

ACTION

Do you live in a "Catholic bubble"? Are all your friends, neighbors, and relatives Catholic? Take a step in faith and get to know someone from another belief or cultural tradition.

PRAYER

Jesus, I like comfort and certainty.
It's easy and convenient for me to
thin-slice people as bad or good,
as a sinner or a saint in the making.
Please open my eyes to the potential
you see in the sinner and help me
to be your love and compassion to
all. Amen.

8

The Woman at the Well

KNOWING AND LOVING

Jesus said to her, "Go, call your husband, and come back." The woman answered him, "I have no husband." Jesus said to her, "You are right in saying, 'I have no husband,' for you have had five husbands, and the one you have now is not your husband. What you have said is true!" The woman said to him, "Sir, I see that you are a prophet. Our ancestors worshiped on this mountain, but you say that the place where people must worship is in Jerusalem." Jesus said to her, "Woman, believe me, the hour is coming when you will worship the Father neither on this mountain nor in Jerusalem. You worship what you do not know; we worship what we know, for salvation is from the Jews. But the hour is coming and is now here when the true worshipers will worship the Father in spirit and truth, for the Father seeks such as these to worship him. God is spirit, and those who worship him must worship in spirit and truth." The woman said to him, "I know that Messiah is coming" (who is called Christ). "When he comes, he will proclaim all things to us." Jesus said to her, "I am he, the one who is speaking to you."...

Then the woman left her water jar and went back to the city. She said to the people, "Come and see a man who told me everything I have ever done! He cannot be the Messiah, can he?"

◆ **JOHN 4:16–26, 28–29**

Cross-References

GENESIS 33:18–20
Jacob buys land and erects an altar

MARK 16:15
After the resurrection, Jesus tells the disciples to preach the good news to all the world

1 CORINTHIANS 9:21–22
Paul says he became as one outside the law to gain those outside the law

Her Story

She is a little put out that this Jewish stranger is there, at Jacob's well, in the middle of the day. This is *her* time. Her alone time. She specifically comes to draw water in the heat of the day.

She once was part of that community of women who came to the well in the morning or early evening, when it was cooler. Besides performing an essential household task, it was an opportunity to catch up with friends, share updates on their families, and exchange a little gossip. But now, she is quite sure, she is a frequent topic of that gossip. So, better to be alone. She knows her life is disordered. She doesn't need their whispers to confirm that.

The stranger can't just sit quietly and let her go about her business. Oh, no. He expects her to get him a drink of water! He gives her some nonsense about "living water," but it's entertaining, in a way, to parry with him. She jokingly asks for this "living water" so she doesn't have to come back again and again to use the well. Wouldn't that be nice?

But then he hits her in the heart: I know you, he says. I know you've had five husbands and now are with a man to whom you're not married. She's rattled by this: how can this stranger know these things and, more importantly, how can this stranger know these things and still be talking with her?

She reverts to detailing their differences. Then she tries once more to bring the conversation to a conclusion: the Messiah will explain it all when he comes.

And the stranger says: "I am he, the one who is speaking to you."

The Messiah? Speaking to *her*? Alone? In the middle of the day? And yet, his face and his eyes have remained friendly throughout this strange conversation.

His friends arrive, and she leaves her water jar and goes into town. All those people who have shunned her and gossiped about her? Suddenly, she is sharing the incident with everyone: he knew all about her life. "He cannot be the Messiah, can he?"

WHAT HAPPENED TO THE WOMAN?

The woman at the well makes her biblical exit after Jesus leaves town. Those in the Eastern Orthodox Church believe she eventually was baptized with the name Photini, which means "the enlightened one." The teaching in that church is that she, two sons, five sisters, and other companions were martyred in Carthage in 66 CE, suffering horrendous tortures but never denying Christ. However, this is not part of the Roman Catholic tradition.

I'd like to think she spent the rest of her life sharing her experience and bringing the good news to Samaritans. She seems to have been transformed by this encounter, leaving her water jar to spread the news to people who likely were anything but friends. That took courage—and belief. It's a powerful thing, hearing that someone knows all about you and loves you...not *anyway* or *in spite of*—just loves you.

But it also may be that the fire Jesus lit inside her burned out after a time and that she went back to getting her water at noon to avoid other women and kept looking for a man or creed she believed would satisfy her more.

WHAT WE CAN LEARN FROM THE WOMAN

It was a two-day walk from Judea to Galilee, and the most direct route was through Samaria, in today's northern West Bank. If you're purely concerned about time—and you're physically fit, for the route is rocky and mountainous—it's the way to go. Cautious Jews of Jesus' time would have modified their trip to avoid Samaria and instead travel through Perea, in the Jordan River valley. Pharisees would have taken the longer road because they didn't like to mess with outsiders and because many Jews and Samaritans despised and distrusted each other. Books have been written about this fracture that occurred centuries before Jesus began his public ministry; the passage of time had done little to heal the enmity.

And yet, in this environment that is hostile on so many fronts, Jesus reveals what, according to John's Gospel, he has never disclosed to anyone but his closest followers: "I am he, the one who is speaking to you."

So—why here? Why now? Why *her*? Why not in Jerusalem or Capernaum or Nazareth or Cana? Why not to those friendly crowds who are starting to gather instead of in this desolate location to a Samaritan—and a Samaritan woman, at that?

Perhaps because she needed him: she needed something and someone to believe in. Perhaps, to her, the fact that he knew all about her, and didn't condemn her or shun her, was just as mind boggling as his statement that he was the Messiah.

Yes, Jesus knows all about you or your spouse or your kids or your friends or those people in your parish who are Christmas-and-Easter-only Catholics. And he still loves every one of us and wants to draw us closer. He'll take whatever belief we can give him, confident that the more time we spend with him, the more time we want to spend with him, the more we'll want to love him. He'll take that chance, just as he did with the woman at the well.

The woman at the well wasn't ready to pronounce to those in the city that Jesus was the Messiah. They probably wouldn't have believed her anyway; after all, her reputation was less than stellar. But they were intrigued when she said what she knew to be truth: Jesus had told her everything about herself. That led them to want to see this man for themselves, and then led to their conversion. The woman at the well provided the "come and see"; Jesus did the heavy lifting and the loving.

A Story
Knowing and Loving

To call my relationship with my first pastor as an adult "stormy" would be an understatement. Father Gerry Creedon ran a loose, volunteer-centric parish, and I liked structure. Loved it, as a matter of fact.

Father Gerry knew a lot about me, due to pastoral counseling and confession. He knew a lot of things my new Catholic friends didn't, and I found it difficult to believe he didn't share some of my profligate history, especially after I learned that my lay "spiritual director" had shared confidences with our prayer group.

Becoming a member of the parish council just one month after returning to the faith provided me with a public venue for arguments with Father Gerry about a great many things, from his off-key serenades at parish events to jokes about my beloved 7:30 AM Mass community's refusal to sing.

The last straw came when on my first Easter back, I volunteered to be a first-time lector and sacristan in addition to my usual usher duties. On the big day, I fell apart. My pages and pages of instructions got jumbled, and I had no idea what was supposed to come next. Our wonderful vicar was the celebrant; he managed to reassign duties on the fly, so the Mass wasn't a total disaster. Instead of thanking the vicar, I lit into Father Gerry when he came into the sacristy to prepare for the next Mass. His patience with me was finally gone, and we screamed at each other for ten minutes.

That's right. I screamed at my pastor. For ten minutes. On Easter Sunday.

We didn't speak to each other for a few weeks. Then I was tapped to host a home Mass for returning Catholics. The organizer arranged for Father Gerry to preside.

There would be around twenty of us. I figured with that many people, it would be easy for Father Gerry and me to avoid each other without anyone else noticing. I prayed for that, anyway.

The evening came, and I was in the kitchen chatting with some of the others when Father Gerry entered. He greeted me as warmly as he ever had. Oh, so we're going to be fake, I thought. I can do that.

Then he said, "I write a bit of poetry. I'm wondering if you'd be willing to help me with that."

I didn't know what to say or think.

After a minute or two of silence, he said, "I really would like to learn from you." Then, turning to the others, he said, "You know, she's quite a good writer. You should read her stuff."

Of course I said yes, and I helped him get a couple of poems pub-

A Deeper Dive

"We are called to rediscover the importance and the sense of our Christian life, initiated in baptism and, like the Samaritan woman, to witness to our brothers [and sisters]. A witness of what? Joy! To witness to the joy of the encounter with Jesus; for, as I said, every encounter with Jesus changes our life, and every encounter with Jesus also fills us with joy, the joy that comes from within. And the Lord is like this. And so we must tell of the marvelous things the Lord can do in our hearts when we have the courage to set aside our own water jar." **POPE FRANCIS, MARCH 23, 2014**[11]

lished. Our relationship was never uncomplicated, but his acceptance of me in full—writer, judgy screamer, uncatechized searcher—was transformational. If Father Gerry could forgive me, I eventually learned, so could God.

A few years later, Father Gerry was assigned to another parish, and we communicated rarely. I'd heard that his beloved brother had died, and I sent a card, albeit late. The day Gerry died, I opened a letter from him I'd received a couple weeks earlier. He thanked me for the card I'd sent—and enclosed a poem he'd written for his brother.

Challenging and Giving Testimony
Saint Olga of Kyiv (c. 890-969)

Olga's conversion to Christianity in the early tenth century probably caused as much gossip as the woman at the well's story of her encounter with Jesus. Probably, that is, if anyone was brave enough to gossip in light of the way that Olga, while still a pagan, avenged the murder of her husband, Prince Igor I.

Igor was killed by a rival tribe, leaving Olga and a three-year-old son. If stories from *The Russian Primary Chronicle*[3] are to be believed, Olga embarked on a multiphase plan of retribution, as evil as it was ingenuous. When the rival tribe invited her to marry their leader, she pretended to consider the invitation. But while she was being presented with the proposal, she had her troops dig a trench under the place where the other tribe's boat was docked, resulting in all of the men being buried alive. Before this became public, she summoned a second group to offer hospitality, only to lock them in a bathhouse and burn it down.

Olga was far from finished. A third group was invited to her husband's pagan funeral. She got them all drunk, then had them killed. Finally, she engineered the destruction of the tribe's headquarters city by tying sulfur to the legs of six pigeons and sprarows, then had the residents who survived killed, enslaved, or pay financial tribute. Her position secured, Olga then ruled the region for about twenty years until her son was crowned.

The circumstances of Olga's conversion are unclear. One saga holds that Constantine VII baptized her about 957 in what is now Istanbul (and includes a likely fanciful tale of how she tricked Constantine into baptizing her so she and her holdings would remain independent of emperor's reach). She also may have converted sometime earlier. Olga did, however, desire to share her new faith with the region. For example, she convinced the holy Roman emperor of the time, Otto I, to send missionaries to the Kyiv area, but they were ultimately unsuccessful as were Olga's efforts to convert her son. Her grandson, Vladimir the Great, converted during his own reign and is credited with the spread of Christianity throughout the area. Perhaps Vladimir's journey was influenced by his grandmother's swath of avenging blood—and the peace she found with Jesus.

Unforgettable You

CONTEMPLATION

Think about or discuss:

- What do you think happened to the woman at the well? What might her life have been like five or ten years after this encounter with Jesus?
- The Sychar community may have scorned the woman for her many marriages and current living situation or perhaps for the outspokenness she shows in her conversation with Jesus. But despite knowing everything about her, Jesus engaged with her as a person with dignity. Consider someone you have turned away from, perhaps with good reason, and what it is in him or her that Jesus finds worthy of redemption.
- What shame or secret are you holding inside, sure that if it is exposed to the light, you will become an outcast? What keeps you from believing you can be forgiven?

ACTION

The woman at the well is a favorite subject for painters and musicians. Olivia Lane's song "Woman at the Well" was featured in the TV series *The Chosen*. Spend some time with the image or music of your choice about this encounter with Christ. Then jot down words about your own encounter or select an image that reminds you of that time and write some verses from John 4:1–42 below it in your scrapbook.

PRAYER

Jesus, I tremble at the thought
of you knowing everything about me.
Help me to believe that you love me,
flawed as I am. Let me open my soul
to trust that with you, I can chart
a course that is pleasing to you. Amen.

CONCLUSION

What do you think happened?

Did the woman at the well keep on evangelizing? Did the widow who offered all she had feel blessed by hearing Jesus' praise? Did the widow at Nain convert everyone she knew by telling of her son's raising from the dead? I wish we could all come together in person and talk about this for hours.

And, what happens to us?

Maybe at this point, you're thinking about moments of grace that changed you profoundly and then lost their luster as "real" life intervened. You love your husband or wife dearly, but sometimes you snap and judge instead of reflecting more deeply. The kids and grandkids are the very greatest gift you've ever received, but it's hard to remember that when they forget your birthday, would prefer to be with their friends, or get into trouble that breaks your heart. You know you make a difference in your day job or ministry, but sometimes it's just plain drudgery, not joy.

We're human. Those days come, and Jesus and his all-embracing love seem very far away. We figure he's got bigger problems to solve than ours or that not even he cannot solve our heartbreaks.

But the Lord loves us in those times of doubt too. And here is the thing: he makes it easy for us to recapture the way our souls flew to him in other conversion moments. The well comes to us. His grace is forever free flowing and rains down on us whether we ask for it or not, whether or not we are ashamed we didn't embrace it more completely earlier. That's how deep and sacrificing the Almighty's love is.

You see, our conversion moments are never "one and done." Jesus is our biggest cheerleader when we surrender even another inch of our souls to grace. He celebrates when we come to him, curious, defeated, desperate, hopeful.

My prayer for you is that you embrace that opportunity for continual conversion, and that you don't despair at the setbacks. Learn from them. Share your journey. Be open to grace whether people know your name or not. He does.

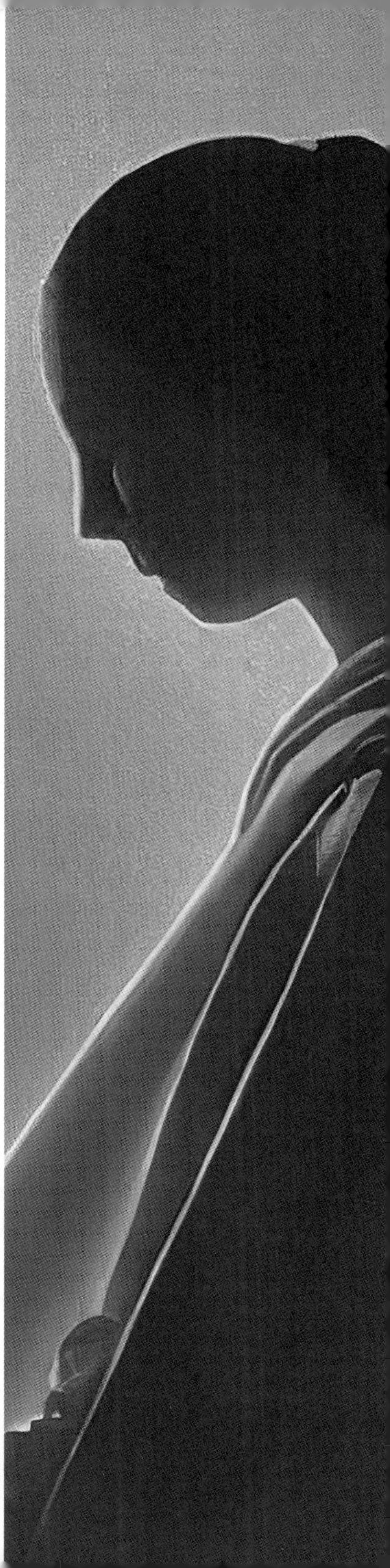

ENDNOTES

1 http://w2.vatican.va/content/john-paul-ii/en/homilies/2001/documents/hf_jp-ii_hom_20010401_nostra-signora-suffragio.html

2 https://uscatholic.org/articles/201603/who-framed-mary-magdalene/

3 https://www.mgh-bibliothek.de/dokumente/a/a011458.pdf

4 https://biblehub.com/sermons/auth/rowland/jesus_lingering_in_the_temple.htm

5 https://www.vatican.va/content/francesco/en/audiences/2016/documents/papa-francesco_20160810_udienza-generale.html

6 https://biblehub.com/sermons/auth/walters/the_infirm_woman_in_the_synagogue.htm

7 https://www.vatican.va/content/francesco/en/angelus/2020/documents/papa-francesco_angelus_20200816.html

8 https://biblehub.com/sermons/auth/maclaren/the_power_of_feeble_faith.htm

9 https://biblehub.com/sermons/auth/glover/the_judges_judged.htm

10 https://biblehub.com/sermons/auth/thomson/she_is_a_sinner.htm

11 https://www.vatican.va/content/francesco/en/angelus/2014/documents/papa-francesco_angelus_20140323.html

ALSO FROM MELANIE RIGNEY

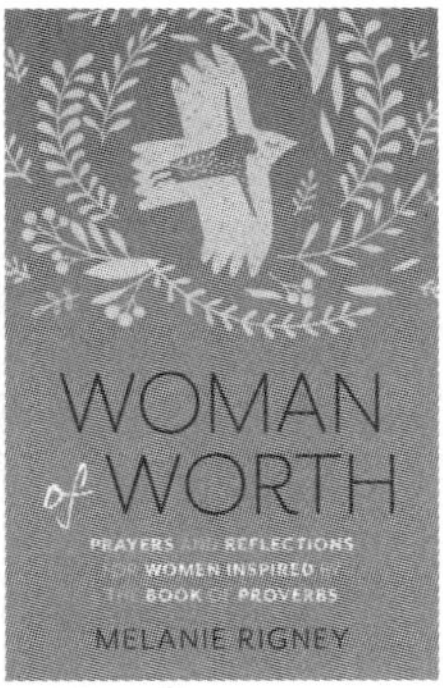

Woman of Worth

Prayers and Reflections for Women Inspired by the Book of Proverbs

Any woman wondering about her worth to her family, to her coworkers, to herself, and to God will find much to rejoice here. Each chapter takes a verse or two from Proverbs 31 and offers a personal story, a reflection on the verse, a portrait of a woman saint who exemplifies the verse, some questions designed for discussion or contemplation, and a prayer. **128 PAGES | $12.95 | 5½" X 8½" | 9781627853385**

The 7 Joys and 7 Sorrows of Mary

Reflections, Actions, and Prayers

In this meaningful new devotional, readers are invited to walk with Mary, the mother of Jesus, as she encounters deep sorrow and great joy throughout her life. From the Annunciation to the Crucifixion and beyond, Melanie Rigney demonstrates how Mary is a model of strength and perseverance for all believers today. These deeply spiritual reflections, prayers, and writing prompts are powerful guides to help us grow closer to both Mary and her Son, Jesus. **32 PAGES | $2.95 | 5½" X 8½" | 9781627857178**

Menopause Moments

A Journal for Nourishing Your Mind, Body, and Spirit in Midlife

This fresh and sanity-saving journal offers nourishing reflections on the many facets of menopause with honesty, understanding, and a touch of humor. Each reflection includes a Scripture passage and a spark for reflection, prayer, and action. This wonderful journal is sure to help you feel refreshed and confident in your future, yourself and your faith. **88 PAGES | $12.95 | 6" X 9" | 9781627856102**

TO ORDER CALL 1-800-321-0411
OR VISIT TWENTYTHIRDPUBLICATIONS.COM

TWENTY-THIRD PUBLICATIONS
A division of Bayard, Inc.